# Jewel

## An Everyday Angel

### An Unauthorized Biography

by Tracey West

SCHOLASTIC INC.
New York  Toronto  London  Auckland  Sydney

*This book could not have been written without the good faith of Bonnie Bader and Craig Walker; the support of Kristin Earhart; the perseverance of Cathleen Bowley and Katherine Noll; the numerological stylings of Judy Noll (for queries or comments for Judy, E-mail her at AliceHalf@aol.com); the encouragement of Shanien Whitaker; the patience of Terry West; and the kindness of everyday angels. Thank you all!*

**Photo credit:**

**front cover photo:** Sandra Johnson/Retna

12 11 10 9 8 7 6 5 4 3 2 1      8 9/9 0 1 2 3/0

Printed in the U.S.A.

First Scholastic printing, March 1998

# Contents

Chapter 1:  A Precious Gem                                    1

Chapter 2:  "Hardwood Grows Slowly"                           5

Chapter 3:  Raised in a Log Cabin                            12

Chapter 4:  Jewel Picks Up a Guitar                          17

Chapter 5:  Van Sweet Van                                    22

Chapter 6:  The Music and the Message                        27

Chapter 7:  EveryDay Angels                                  35

Chapter 8:  A Win, a Loss, and
            an Unforgettable Dress                           40

Chapter 9:  The Loves of Her Life                            43

Chapter 10:  A Very Good Year                                47

Chapter 11:  Straight from
             the Star's Mouth                                54

Chapter 12:  Jewel's Personality
             Profile                                         58

Chapter 13:  Jewel from A to Z                               64

Chapter 14:  Where to Find Jewel                             70

Chapter 15:  Jewel's Discography                             74

# 1

## A Precious Gem

The spotlight is on. Jewel stands before the microphone, ready to sing her hit single "Foolish Games" at the 1997 MTV Movie Awards. Until this moment, the crowd has been gawking at celebrities and cracking up at host Mike Myers. But now all eyes are on Jewel, and the mumblings have all died down.

As Jewel sings, it's clear that her heart is in every passionate word. It's a striking performance, and when the last chords fade away the audience bursts into astonished applause. Once again, Jewel has made her mark. It's another defining moment in her short but tremendously successful career.

Robert Shapiro, executive vice president of Jewel's record company, Atlantic Records, has seen her make magic with "Foolish Games" before. "I've been seeing her in concert for two years," he told *Billboard* magazine in 1997. "The silence and then the hysteria that follow this

1

song have always been one of the most provocative moments of her show. If you're not crying, you're just standing there stunned."

"Foolish Games" may have been the highlight of the MTV Movie Awards, but it's just one highlight in the young singer's life. Since her album, *Pieces of You*, debuted in 1995, Jewel has sold millions of albums, toured half the world, acquired legions of devoted fans, and even appeared on the cover of *Time* magazine! What is it about the girl from Alaska that's made her such a superstar? Like a precious gem, Jewel has many facets:

• **She Sure Can Sing:** Jewel's voice is one that grabs your heart and just won't let go. It's sweet and strong at the same time, and it often changes depending on the mood of the song. Critics have compared her to folksingers Joni Mitchell and Tracy Chapman.

• **She's Got a Way With Words:** Jewel's lyrics and poetry (which can be found on the sleeve of her CD) seem to speak directly to her fans, especially young listeners struggling with relationships, their parents, and decisions about the future. It makes sense — Jewel wrote the songs on her CD when she was a teenager.

• **She Knows How to Put on a Show:** Atlantic Records credits Jewel's live performances with putting the singer on the map. It's one thing to hear Jewel's CD, but to see her perform is a whole different experience. She makes an impression that most fans can never forget. "What sells you about her is [seeing her] live," John Knapp, program director at WPLY radio, told *Billboard*. "She's very witty and connects with her audience."

• **She's Got a Very Good Head on Her Shoulders:** Growing up without electricity and a TV meant that Jewel had a chance to fill her head with stuff other than sitcoms and commercials. Jewel thinks a lot about life and encourages her fans to do the same. She also thinks it's important for people to care about one another and the world around them.

• **She's Got Personality:** Just because Jewel is smart doesn't mean she's a bore. During shows, she makes jokes and sometimes even does impressions between songs. And you never know what she'll say in interviews. When a reporter from the Gannett News Service called her in 1995, she answered the phone with a long "Meeeeeeeoooooow." What a way to say hello!

• **She Works Hard:** Whether canning salmon with her family after school, or performing forty shows in one month, Jewel always gives one hundred percent. No matter how tired she got on the road to stardom, Jewel never gave up.

- **She's Beautiful:** Fans know that Jewel is a beautiful person on the inside, but the world can't help noticing that she's gorgeous on the outside, too. There's no denying that Jewel's pretty, heart-shaped face, hazel eyes, and sweet smile have helped to win over more than a few fans!

When you combine all of these qualities into one person, you end up with a precious, glittering gem — a real Jewel! No matter what the future holds for her, she's already made a huge impact on the music industry — and in the lives of many of her fans.

# 2
# "Hardwood Grows Slowly"

July 1995. Jeff Spevak, the Gannett reporter whom Jewel greeted with a "Meeeeoooooow," caught her on *Live With Regis and Kathie Lee*. Spevak loved Jewel's performance. But in a news article the next day, he compared her to megastar Michael Jackson: "Her new album, *Pieces of You*, will not sell 50 million copies. It won't sell a million," he predicted.

Spevak was wrong. *Pieces* went on to sell a lot more than a million copies — over seven million by the end of 1997. But when Jeff Spevak made his prediction, there probably weren't too many people who would have disagreed with him. Jewel's album had been released six months before, and hadn't made a big splash. In fact, it took about a year and a half for the album to become a hit. During that time, Jewel worked hard to promote the album, and Atlantic Records supported her all the way.

Here's a look at how Jewel went from folk-singer to superstar in eighteen months:

## Winter–Spring 1995

After Jewel was discovered singing at the Innerchange coffeehouse in San Diego, California, Atlantic Records signed her up. Jewel's album, *Pieces of You,* was released in February 1995.

Atlantic sent Jewel on a whirlwind tour of coffeehouses. The dates started to earn her more fans, but record sales were relatively small — about 500 CDs a week, Atlantic Records' Robert Shapiro told *Billboard.*

In May, Jewel made the leap from the small stage to the small screen. She appeared on *Late Night with Conan O'Brien* and sang "Who Will Save Your Soul." After that night, her sales jumped about 1,900 CDs a week. The public was starting to take notice.

## Summer–Fall 1995

Atlantic kept Jewel busy with spots on television and radio shows. She went from playing coffeehouses to opening for some of Atlantic's other acts: gothic rocker Peter Murphy, and the band Deep Blue Something (best known for their single "Breakfast at Tiffany's").

But touring that summer wasn't easy for Jewel. Because Jewel's music was so different from Peter Murphy's, Murphy's fans often booed Jewel when she was on stage. "I wanted to kill myself after every show," she later told *Rolling Stone*.

And fans eager to hear "Breakfast at Tiffany's" would yell, "We want Deep Blue Something!" when Jewel was trying to sing. And in Detroit, kids arrived at her show expecting to see rap star Jewell. By the end of the show, the entire audience was almost gone.

Jewel never forgot what that felt like. Later in her career, fans were screaming *her name* during opening act David Baerwald's set at a show in Connecticut. That made Jewel upset. "Be nice to opening acts, people," she advised in the *Hartford Courant*.

Putting up with boos and rude fans soon paid off. In November 1995, Jewel started getting lots of attention. *Pieces of You* finally hit the Billboard charts, and Jewel made two big — and very different — TV appearances.

The night after Thanksgiving, TNT aired a special stage performance of *The Wizard of Oz* — starring Jewel in the role of Dorothy! Jewel joined Nathan Lane, Roger Daltrey, Debra Winger, Natalie Cole, and Jackson Browne in the performance, which was a benefit for the Children's Defense Fund.

Because she grew up without a TV, Jewel

hadn't seen the movie until just before performing in the show. But that didn't stop her from bringing the classic to life.

"It was a big mouthful to have that big of a script and to have two dance routines," she remembered in an interview with *This Is the Sound*. "But if water seeks its own level I couldn't go wrong, because all you can do is rise to the occasion."

Co-star Jackson Browne, who played the Scarecrow, had nice things to say about Jewel. "She's a really fresh, exciting talent," he told the New York *Daily News*.

Ten million viewers watched Jewel sing and dance her way down the yellow brick road that night. At the very same time, other viewers were getting to see a different side of Jewel. She appeared on the VH1 program *Duets* with Melissa Etheridge.

Jewel's doubleheader that night made many people sit up and take notice. The next month, she was making waves on *Entertainment Tonight* and *The Tonight Show With Jay Leno*. What a way to end the year!

## Winter–Spring 1996

Jewel started off the new year with a red-white-and-blue bang, performing at one of President Clinton's inaugural balls. Around the same time, "Who Will Save Your Soul" was getting radio airplay again, thanks to the Jay Leno appearance and a push from VH1.

When the single was first released a year before, many radio stations didn't play it. "Many program directors said it didn't sound like anything on the radio and wasn't playable," Atlantic Records' Rob Shapiro explained in *Billboard*.

Lesley Fram, assistant program director of WNNX Atlanta, was one of those people. But, in time, she came around. "Because of the quality of the song, we decided to try it," she told *Billboard*. Other radio stations agreed, and the song soon became a Top 40 hit.

Jewel was still an opening act, but she was getting much better gigs. In April, she joined legendary rocker Bob Dylan for five shows on his tour.

By the end of April, *Pieces* was selling 22,000 copies a week — the best sales of her career.

Things were looking good, but Jewel was still cautious. "I'm trying to be realistic," she told *People* magazine in May. "What's happening to me now could end tomorrow, and I'd be back where I was."

One week later, Jewel became a headliner in her own right. Now she had her own opening act — Duncan Sheik. Atlantic Records broadcast their May 16 show live on the Internet. That night, 272,000 people logged on, breaking the company's record.

"Many 'a star is born' comments were heard that night," Atlantic Records boasted in a press release.

Atlantic may have sounded like a proud parent, but it was right. A star *was* born. In August, "Who Will Save Your Soul" peaked on the *Billboard* charts at number 11. A month later, *Pieces of You* went platinum (selling one million copies). Jewel toured for three weeks with another legendary rocker, Neil Young. It had taken a year and a half, but Jewel was now a certified superstar.

The road to stardom may have been bumpy — and even paved with yellow bricks. And it was a tiring road. Jewel told *Billboard* that she played live 800 times in 1996! That's more than twice every single day of the year. But Jewel wouldn't have it any other way.

Early in her career, she told the Gannett News Service, Neil Young inspired her to think about the long journey in a new way. "Hardwood grows slowly," Jewel explained. "Wood like cedar grows very fast, [but] it's very soft. The technology is so good these days, an artist can grow very fast, but they also die faster. I want to build up fans slowly."

And when she did have those fans, Jewel told *Billboard*, "I'm very pleased it's taken as long as it has. I've always wanted to be a long-term career artist, which never means hitting it big right away from the first album. The kids that are with me and have been with me from the beginning are there because I'm speaking to their hearts. Cleverness only speaks to the clever. If you speak from the heart, then you have the chance to have people feel moved and changed."

By the end of 1996, Jewel had already moved and changed millions of fans. And she was just getting started!

# 3

## Raised in a Log Cabin

Jewel describes her rise to fame as like the growth of a hardwood tree. Every tree starts with a seed. And for Jewel, that seed was planted in Alaska.

If you were to visit the area where it all began, you'd need to head to south central Alaska. Jewel grew up there, about eleven miles away from the town of Homer. The pretty little village sits on the shores of Kachemak Bay. The scenery is breathtakingly beautiful. Icy glaciers jut out of the distant water. The majestic Kenai Mountains rise into the blue sky.

Alaska is a pretty cold place, but Homer is spared the worst of it. Thanks to the mountains, which protect the town from severe cold, the temperature rarely goes below zero degrees Fahrenheit in the winter. Then again, it usually doesn't get much warmer than 70 degrees in the summertime!

Jewel told *Rolling Stone* that Homer is "very

cosmopolitan and artistic. And just a funny little town."

Homer didn't start out as artistic. The first Europeans to settle in Homer were prospectors looking for gold in the 1800s. They didn't find any gold, but some stuck around anyway. Decades later, in the 1960s, artists and radicals moved to Homer. Today, the town has a reputation as an arts colony. Every spring, Homer holds an arts festival that lasts for a whole month.

The practice of homesteading is popular in the Homer area. The Homestead Act was in effect from 1862 to 1977. It said that a person could pay a small fee and get up to 160 acres of land owned by the government. All they had to do was make some improvements to the land and live on it for at least five years.

Jewel was born in 1974 and grew up on a homestead near Homer. Her grandfather, Yule Kilcher, started the homestead when he moved to Alaska from Switzerland as a young man. Jewel's father, Atz Kilcher, and her mother, Nedra Carroll, raised their family in a log cabin on the homestead.

Life on the homestead wasn't easy. Jewel shared a room with her two brothers. There was no electricity or running water in the cabin. That meant no TV, no shower, and an icy outhouse instead of an indoor bathroom.

The Kilchers lived off the land. They raised cows for meat and caught salmon. They grew vegetables in their garden. Each day began at five A.M. so that chores could be done before school started. Getting to school was another ordeal — Jewel had to walk three miles, even in the freezing cold!

"It was like pioneers, when people moved west," Jewel explained to *Rolling Stone.* "We had a hose, and you hooked it up to the stream. But if there were worms because the stream flooded, there were worms in your faucet."

Jewel told the magazine that while other kids were watching cartoons after school, she and her brothers would be canning salmon. "It was hard work," said Jewel. "But I was also very proud of it, and it shaped me into a certain kind of person."

The hard work had its rewards. "I got to ride my horse and find God and simplicity," Jewel told New York *Newsday.* "I know my place in nature and I know myself in silence."

Working the land shaped Jewel's personality. At the same time, her parents were helping Jewel to shape her talent. Atz and Nedra performed together as folksingers. When Jewel was about six years old, they brought her into the act. They sang for crowds in hotels and Eskimo villages.

Young Jewel was happy performing. "I don't

recall Jewel ever being daunted by a crowd. She loves people," Jewel's mother told *People* magazine in 1996.

It was during those days that Jewel learned her most infamous skill — yodeling. Yodeling started in Switzerland, and Atz was skilled at it. Six-year-old Jewel picked it up quickly — which is pretty amazing for someone so young — and the yodeling became a part of the act. Today, Jewel still yodels at live shows, usually at the request of her fans.

When Jewel was eight, she went through her first big change in life. Atz and Nedra divorced in 1982.

"For a child, divorce is like being torn out of the only air you've ever known, and you're suddenly in a very strange climate," Jewel is quoted as saying in *Twist* magazine. To deal with her feelings, Jewel started writing them down.

Jewel stayed on the homestead with her father and continued to perform with him.

In an interview with the New Jersey *Bergen Record,* Jewel remembered those days. "My father insisted on professionalism," she said. "His belief was that if people were paying money to see us, we had to be the best we could be and we rehearsed all the time striving for that perfection."

While Jewel was rising to the challenges of performing, she was facing another challenge in school. Jewel suffers from dyslexia, a common disorder that makes reading difficult.

*BOP!* magazine reported Jewel's thoughts on struggling with the problem. "Having dyslexia made me feel like I would never be interested in life again," Jewel said. "I used to love reading when I was little, and then it became difficult and I didn't understand why. I thought, 'What a bummer, my passion all drained out of me.' So when I found out I had dyslexia, it was like, oh, that's what it was."

For all of the hard work and rehearsals, Jewel remembers her days in Alaska fondly. She told *Newsday* that she carries rocks and eagle feathers from Alaska with her. And in an interview with *Alaska Center,* she revealed, "I carry a Tupperware of dirt from the farm and when it starts getting too thick, I just open it and smell the earth."

If Jewel is like a tree, then it's clear that her roots are firmly planted in the Alaskan soil where she grew up.

# 4
## Jewel Picks Up a Guitar

With working on the homestead, yodeling for crowds, dealing with her parents' divorce, and struggling with dyslexia, Jewel experienced more when she was a kid than most people do in a lifetime. But she was just getting started. Jewel's teen years would be just as eventful.

Jewel seems to have had fun during her early years of high school. She went through a stage when she started dressing in the style of the 1940s. After that stage, she changed styles and joined a rap group called La Creme.

Soon after, Jewel got restless. She became "adopted" by a Native American tribe. That experience helped shape Jewel's personal views on spirituality.

After ninth grade, Jewel went to live with relatives in Hawaii. The sunny island shores couldn't have been more different from the life she left behind. But she had a hard time getting along there and only stayed for a year. When she returned to Alaska, she went to live with her mother in Anchorage, Alaska's largest city. From Anchorage, Jewel and Nedra moved to Seward, a town about the same size as Homer and not too far away.

Jewel could have finished high school in her home state, but another opportunity knocked. She was offered a scholarship to the Michigan boarding school, Interlochen Center for the Arts, which teaches the arts to high school students from all over the world. At Interlochen, Jewel would have the chance to study voice training with professionals.

Even with the scholarship, though, the Kilchers still needed an additional 11,000 dollars for the tuition fee. Where most families would have given up, the Kilchers rose to the occasion. Jewel's mother organized a benefit show and auction to raise the money. The events were a success, and Jewel headed out to Interlochen at the start of her junior year.

The first time she set eyes on the school, Jewel probably felt right at home. Interlochen is tucked into Michigan's northern woods, right in between two lakes. Some of the buildings look like log cabins, and others look like they're made of stone. "It's very rustic and pristine," says Interlochen's Dee Smith.

As much as Interlochen looked like home, it was an eye-opening experience for Jewel.

"My two years there were a turning point. I saw a bigger world. I immersed myself in everything — drama, dance, sculpture, music," she reported in *Faces in Pop*.

At Interlochen, Jewel studied voice. She took classes in opera and performed in the choir. She also worked at the school, modeling for the sculpture students and shoveling clay dust from the sculpting studios.

"The things I had been taught at home, the discipline, the value of hard work, they all helped when I got to Interlochen. There were kids there who didn't even know how to shovel," Jewel remembered in the *Bergen Record*.

But a shovel wasn't the most important thing Jewel picked up in Interlochen — it was a guitar.

*Faces in Pop* reported that Jewel said, "I was sixteen or seventeen during my senior year at Interlochen when I first started studying the guitar and getting serious about my songwriting."

Learning the guitar presented Jewel with another challenge. Dyslexia can affect other skills besides reading. Jewel found she had to give an extra effort to learn the instrument.

"Because of my history, it's hard for me to learn things, so I practiced twenty times as hard," she explained in *Rolling Stone*.

Jewel practiced her guitar whenever she got the chance. Interlochen art instructor Jean Parsons remembers, "She just sort of walked into the art department and wanted to be the sculpture model. She became very good friends with all the kids in the art department. She was a very patient model for us. I think what made it workable for her is that she brought her guitar in and practiced while she posed. Jewel was composing a lot of songs at that point. So all the day classes, the evenings, and weekends, I would say really helped her do a lot of composing."

Of course, you don't find many opera singers playing the guitar. Jewel was beginning to find that opera just wasn't for her.

"I found that opera improved my falsetto, but sort of diminished the joy of letting it flow," she said in an interview with *Alaska Center*.

One of Jewel's voice instructors, Nicole Philibosian, remembers, "Vocally, I just tried to keep her on track and helped teach her how to sing high notes. We're pretty open, but we don't teach blues or pop singing, but here she was, so what were we going to do with her? We taught her what we could. And we're very glad she was here."

Another of Jewel's voice instructors, Ron Gentry, says, "She was a real maverick and she knew exactly where she was going."

And while Jewel was learning new skills, she continued to polish an old favorite. "She yodeled all the time," sculpting instructor Jean Parsons recalls. "That was very commonplace."

It was at Interlochen that Jewel got a taste of her future — performing her own songs and playing her own guitar.

Nicole Philibosian was lucky enough to see one of Jewel's early performances. "Jewel was just getting ready to leave Interlochen and she said, 'I'm going to sing in Traverse City tonight, do you want to come hear me?' She was singing at a coffeehouse, playing her guitar. Jewel just blew me away. I just sat there with tears coming down my cheeks."

Jewel left Interlochen in 1992, ready to share her music with the world. When she graduated, she joined the ranks of Interlochen alumni such as cartoonist Cathy Guisewite, opera star Jessye Norman, and TV journalist Mike Wallace. Four years later, Jewel would become just as famous as any of them — if not more so.

"Jewel would be our all-time biggest [graduate], since she made the cover of *Time* magazine," says Dee Smith.

She's got a point. But as her fans know, after leaving Interlochen Jewel still had a way to go before her face would be seen on newsstands around the country.

# 5

## Van Sweet Van

After graduating from Interlochen, Jewel hopped on a train to San Diego. Her mom, Nedra, was working there as a glass artist. Jewel wasn't sure exactly what to do with her future.

"Until I started finding my direction, my time in San Diego was a difficult time for me," she says in *Faces in Pop*. "I felt a lot of social pressure to figure out what I was going to do with the rest of my life. I had no desire to go to college, but I also felt no peace in traveling or just bumming around. I got a number of dead-end jobs . . . got fired a couple of times. I was frightened and a little depressed. The idea of spending my life in a nine-to-five job made me feel trapped and hopeless."

Jewel tried waitressing as a way to help her mom pay the rent and the bills. According to Jewel's official Web site, she could never figure her customers' bills correctly. Jewel thinks it might have been because of her dyslexia, but she also admits she never had a chance to become comfortable with math. That's because her math teacher used to throw her out of class for yodeling!

After Jewel got fired from her waitressing job, she made a big decision — one that would change the course of her life. Jewel decided that struggling to make money wasn't worth it if she had to do something she hated. She knew she could make some money by singing and playing her guitar, but not enough to pay the rent. So she took a giant step. She moved out of the apartment, and into a van!

"I told myself, 'Okay, I'm going to do something I love or I'm going to die,'" she reported to *People* magazine.

Jewel's mom bought her own van, and the two often parked side by side. Jewel remembered those days in an interview at the CBS Grammy Awards preview show: "I got fired from my last job and that was it. My mom was, like, we're just going to do what we love, and we're gonna just have faith. So I lived in my van, and she lived in her van. And I decided . . . I want to do what I love only. I love singing. I never really thought I could make a living at it, it was dreaming."

In many ways, van life was much harder than life on the homestead. In Alaska, Jewel had a home. Now she was homeless. She survived by eating carrots and peanut butter, but she was often hungry. She washed her hair in the rest room sinks at restaurants. Sometimes, she would hear people muttering about the homeless, just loud enough for her to hear.

Still, in many ways, the days in the van were also wonderful. In her poem "Upon Moving Into My Van," Jewel writes: *Joy. Pure Joy. I am / What I always wanted to grow up and be.*

Life was simple. Jewel wrote songs, and surfed in the Pacific Ocean. And the freedom of van living allowed her to enjoy the beauty of San Diego with her mother. "We both had favorite places to park. She preferred someplace by the ocean. I had a little tree that bloomed year-round, and I would park my van next to it and open up the curtain so its flowers would spill into the window. Or I would park wherever the surf was good," *Twist* magazine quoted Jewel as saying.

Through it all, Jewel worked on her music, and she was really getting good. The *Orange County Register* reported that during this time, Jewel met Flea of the Red Hot Chili Peppers. Flea bumped into Jewel, and she played him a song on her guitar. Flea was impressed. He predicted she'd soon be a star.

But Jewel still had one more stop on the road to stardom. That was the Innerchange coffeehouse in San Diego. Jewel worked out a deal to

24

play at the club every Thursday night. "They said I could keep the door money, and they would keep the coffee sales," she told LAUNCH-online.

Before long, word of mouth spread about the folksinger with a voice like an angel. Thursday nights at the Innerchange became crowded with fans. Jewel was at a high point. She told *Alaska Center* that while singing there, "I prayed I would be given the chance to live my life doing what made me happy and maybe by living my dream I could cause others to remember theirs."

In *Cosmopolitan,* Jewel recalled, "I truly felt, God, life doesn't get any better than this. I never meant to land a record deal. I never thought I was good enough."

But lots of people *did* think Jewel was good enough. Soon scouts from record labels were checking out Jewel's shows at the Innerchange. When Atlantic Records offered her a contract, it was like a dream come true. It wasn't long before Jewel said good-bye to her van days for good.

Does she miss those days? "I don't miss starving. I don't miss stealing toilet paper," she told *This Is the Sound.* "Living in a van was a freedom. I think I led more of a free life then in some respects than I do now, but I'm so much more fulfilled."

And Jewel definitely doesn't worry as much as

she used to. "These days, I wake up giggling every morning," she said in 1996 in *Scholastic Update*.

With worries about money and getting enough to eat far behind her, Jewel was free to concentrate on her first passion — her music.

# 6

# The Music and the Message

When "Who Will Save Your Soul" started getting regular airplay, listeners sat up and took notice. Maybe it was Jewel's rich, beautiful voice. Maybe it was the fact that her lyrics seemed to be saying something. Most likely, it was a combination of the two.

To understand what it is that makes Jewel such a gem, it's important to look at her singing, her songwriting, and the songs that touched our hearts.

## The Singing

It should come as no surprise that the suits at Atlantic Records are the first to praise Jewel's voice.

"She has one of the most God-given voices I have ever heard an artist be given," executive vice president and general manager Robert Shapiro told *Rolling Stone*.

Another executive, Andrea Ganis, is more

descriptive. "Her vocal power is so extraordinary; it really shows off the fact that she can sing the roof off the building," she told *Billboard*.

Shapiro and Ganis may sound like cheerleaders, but the critics agree with them. In a 1997 review, a reporter for the New York *Daily News* wrote, "A . . . reason for Jewel's popularity is her voice, a high, supple instrument that can give her tunes spring and charm." The reporter, like many others, compared Jewel's voice to legendary folk-rock singer Joni Mitchell.

Other critics have pointed out that Jewel's voice changes from song to song. One minute she can sound light and airy, like Joni Mitchell, but the next minute she'll surprise you with a throaty growl that sounds more like Tracy Chapman.

Jewel explained her vocal style in an interview with the *Los Angeles Times*. "I get bored easily, so when I sing, I have to change character," she said. "If you sing in the same voice, people tend not to hear the words because it becomes monotonous. To me [singing] is about shape and tension and color."

Jewel has said that she's more comfortable with her singing than with her guitar playing. That certainly makes sense. After all, she's been singing since she was six years old. She didn't pick up a guitar until her senior year of high school.

Jewel — music's brightest gem.

During Jewel's senior year of high school at Interlochen, where she majored in voice.

Music isn't Jewel's only love — she also likes to brave the waves.

Jewel was still getting used to being in the spotlight when she performed at New York City's Irving Plaza in May 1996.

With B.B. King and Busta Rhymes after the announcement of the 1996 Grammy nominees.

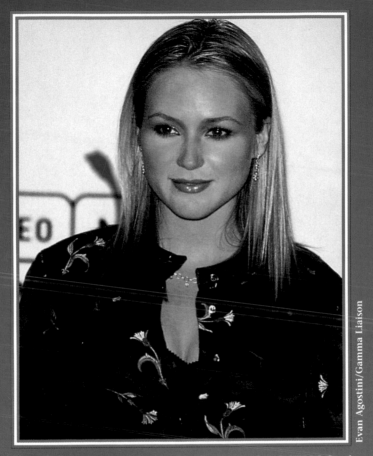

Jewel dressed with Asian flair at the MTV Music Awards, and took home the best female video award for "You Were Meant for Me."

Jewel tunes her guitar at the Blockbuster Rock Festival.

A captivating, candlelit performance at Wiltern
Theatre in Louisiana.

Two stars of the Lilith main stage, Jewel and
Sheryl Crow.

Eddie Malluk

Jay Blakesberg/Retna

"I feel most myself when I am onstage, when I'm singing or when I'm writing."
—Jewel, *Rolling Stone*

Jewel gives her
young fans
a thumbs-up at
the Kids Choice
Awards.

Jewel, Alec Baldwin, and other celebrities
support the National Endowment
for the Arts at a fund-raising gala in
Washington, DC.

At the American Music Awards, Jewel dazzled the crowd and thanked them for their support as she accepted the award for favorite new pop/rock artist.

In Paris with Sean Penn.

At the 1997 MTV Movie Awards
with her boyfriend, Michel.

Jewel is very focused and completely at ease when she plays in concert.

Her lyrics are poetic and honest, and she sings from the heart.

"I'm very lucky to be doing what I love."
—**Jewel,** *Bergen Record*

"My voice is more true to my thought process. I know my voice. I've played with it a lot. It's an instrument I have command over," she told the *Bergen Record* early in 1997.

If there is one criticism made about Jewel's voice, it is that her vocals are much more powerful at live performances than they are on *Pieces of You.*

"I was getting constant comments that, 'Jewel, you sing so much better live than on your album.'" she told *Billboard.* "I've got more comfortable with recording in the studio."

Anyone who's compared the single "You Were Meant for Me" on the album to the re-recorded single knows that Jewel is indeed becoming more comfortable in the studio. The vocals on the new single are strong, clear, and beautiful.

In a LAUNCHonline interview, she explained, "I sing better in front of people. I get a better vocal performance. Being a studio artist is a different beast, a different animal. I've gotten more comfortable with it over the years; it's the same with my guitar playing."

While fans eagerly wait to hear Jewel's vocals on her second album, they can still hear her at her live shows. There is no question that *Pieces of You* owes a lot of its success to Jewel's many live performances.

"My sales are purely from touring," Jewel told *YM* in 1997.

*Entertainment Weekly* pinpointed another reason why fans love to see Jewel live. "Charisma isn't a given for folkies, but Jewel has it," the magazine wrote.

## The Songwriting

For Jewel, writing songs has always been about more than penning a catchy tune. Her lyrics are about making people think about their lives and the world around them.

"Music touches people's hearts," Jewel explained at the CBS Grammy Awards preview show. "You know, it doesn't go through your mental capacity, it just moves you and it will let you cry. It's worth it doing a show and when you touch a crowd and move yourself at the same time. You change lives and you change the world."

In order to change lives, you've got to understand people. Many of Jewel's songs were inspired by observing the people around her.

In *Time* magazine, Jewel talked about what she wanted her songs to accomplish. "There was an innocence that prevailed in the sixties that was crushed by the assassination of JFK and [Martin Luther] King. Our parents have become disillusioned. It is their disillusionment we deal with in many ways; it's a kind of crust we have to break through. People are hungry for emotiveness. They want honesty, emotional blood-and-bone honesty."

Writing songs with blood-and-bone honesty is no easy task. But it's something Jewel has strived for. "I used to not be able to speak, to articulate my heart. I've gotten better at speaking from my heart honestly," Jewel told the *Los Angeles Times*.

## The Songs

Here's the story behind some of the songs on *Pieces of You*:

• "Who Will Save Your Soul": Jewel's first hit was the third song she ever wrote. She was only 17 when she wrote it. In fact, Jewel was between the ages of 17 and 19 when she wrote *all* of the songs on the album.

The song takes a critical look at the way modern people live life, concerned about money and getting ahead but never really living. "Who will save your soul if you won't save your own?" Jewel asks. In *Billboard*, Jewel explains that she was inspired to write the lyrics on arrival in Los Angeles after a short trip singing in the streets of Mexico. The "lonely concrete" of the big city made an impression on her.

• "You Were Meant for Me": Co-written with then-boyfriend Steve Poltz, the song is about as close to a popular love song as Jewel gets on the album. Of course, it's bittersweet, as Jewel wistfully sings of her unrequited love. "I try and tell myself it'll be all right. I just shouldn't think anymore tonight."

Jewel recorded the single a total of three times. The first time was for the album. The second time, Atlantic Records wanted to try a new mix, with more guitar. They did, and Jewel hated the result. So it was back in the studio again and, as the saying goes, the third time was the charm. "You Were Meant for Me" reached number one on *Billboard*'s Hot 100 Airplay chart. The chart-topping version is the one you hear on the radio and in the video.

• "Foolish Games": Jewel's third hit single began as a poem she wrote when she was sixteen. Like "You Were Meant for Me," this song was re-recorded for the single.

"When I was recording *Pieces of You*, I never thought anybody would hear these songs," Jewel told *Billboard*. "This gave me a second chance to do what I thought was justice to the song."

• "Pieces of You": The single that gave the album its name is a look at the psychology of hatred. "Ugly girl, do you hate her because she's pieces of you?" Jewel asks. Quick-thinking

Jewel used the song to teach a lesson to a rude audience member at a live show in 1997. The *Daily News* reported that a boy was shouting during Jewel's set, so she sang "Pieces" and added a line about "stupid boys" who wreck her songs. Lyrics are the best revenge!

• "Daddy": This song, about a girl's feelings toward her racist father, is definitely *not* about Atz Kilcher, Jewel's daddy.

"My poor father. We live in a small town in Alaska and everyone thinks it's about him," Jewel told Lauren Hutton in a television interview. The song is really about the father of a friend that Jewel knew when she was a kid.

• "I'm Sensitive": Another song with a message, this sweet song gives some insight into Jewel's character. "Maybe if we are surrounded in beauty/Someday we will become what we see," Jewel sings. This song is also notable for inspiring the name that Jewel's fans give themselves, the EveryDay Angels (more on them in the next chapter).

• "Amen": This song closes the album much in the same way the word is used to end a prayer. Jewel has stated that this is her favorite song, because the lyrics deal with how "we become what we're told [we're going to become]," she revealed in *Cosmopolitan*.

So what *does* make Jewel such a gem? It's a potent combination of a beautiful voice, a charismatic personality, and a unique ability to touch people's hearts with her lyrics. As the singer herself might say, "Amen."

# 7

## EveryDay Angels

"There's a lot I'd like to do for the world and I think music is a wonderful medium to do it through because it touches people's hearts more than their minds," Jewel told *Newsday* in 1996. It's clear that the singer has influenced her fans in many real ways.

Jewel began by reaching one fan at a time. In 1995, she told *The Record* that she had recently talked to a man after one of her shows. He told Jewel that he used to write poetry, but he had given it up. After seeing Jewel live, though, he started writing it again. "This is what makes this all so worthwhile," Jewel said of the incident, "the fact that I can touch someone and help rekindle their dreams."

As Jewel's fan base grew, so did her influence on them. Many turn to Jewel for advice and her thoughts on life. That's a big responsibility, but Jewel takes it seriously.

"My fans are very polite. People come to my

shows with signs that say, 'Maintaining our Innocence'," she told *Rolling Stone*. "I just want to tell kids, come on man, get excited! There have always been wars and pollution and poverty, but we're at the most unique time in the history of humanity to do something about it. We're worrying less about survival, and more and more about what is our spirit. Every kid is asking me about that right now."

It's amazing that so many fans have responded to Jewel's music and her philosophies on life. But perhaps even more amazing than that is the way that Jewel's fans have banded together in a way that few fans ever do.

It all began around 1995, when fans of Jewel formed a newsgroup on the Internet. The sent messages to one another, gave details of shows they had seen, and shared their feelings about Jewel. They called themselves the EveryDay Angels, after lyrics from the song "I'm Sensitive": "We are everyday angels/Be careful with me 'cause I'd like to stay that way."

Usually, most newsgroups never expand beyond the Internet. But early in 1996, the EDAs (as they say for short) began to meet in person.

"We became very close friends," says Dennis Harris. "Someone once posted to the list that we started out as fans of Jewel, and became fans of each other." The forty-year-old from Massachusetts explained that he first saw Jewel in *The*

*Wizard of Oz*, and then became interested in her music. He liked what Jewel had to say. "She has a great head on her shoulders, and her message is one of hope and inspiration."

This message motivated EDA, and they started seeing each other more often, getting together at shows or at one of the members' homes. It wasn't uncommon for forty people to show up for an EDA weekend.

Jewel was appreciative of the EDAs, and in 1996 she made a special effort to thank them. She held a free concert for EDA members just outside of Woodstock, New York, where she was working on recording her second album. Over two hundred fans came from all over the country. The EDA organized an effort called "Angel Needs a Ride" (named after a Jewel song) to make sure everyone could get there. The event soon became known as "Jewelstock."

The night after the show, Jewel held another concert, this time with a fifteen dollar ticket price. Proceeds went to benefit a local theater.

Jewelstock showed fans that when people band together, they can accomplish great things. That's when the EDA really got going. In early 1997, they started talking about finding ways to use their numbers to make a difference in the world. Jewel encouraged them further. Before her 1997 birthday, members of the group asked her what she wanted to get. Jewel replied over the Internet that she didn't need anything, but she thought it would be great if her fans could help each other or make donations to others in her name.

The EDA took Jewel's words to heart, organizing a blood drive and donating blood in Jewel's name. Other fans reached out to the victim of a car accident. Not only did they help raise $40,000 for a specially equipped van that would accommodate the needs of the wheelchair-bound young man, they became his friends.

The fans decided they wouldn't stop there. More and more of them found different ways to volunteer.

In 1997, the EDA found a very special way to thank Jewel for her inspiration. It started with a fan in Montreal, who wanted to register a star in Jewel's name. The EDA raised the money, and up in the sky somewhere is a star with the name "Jewel Kilcher — Star of the North."

By the end of 1997, some members of the EDA took their commitment to helping others a step further. Dennis Harris and other members of the EDA officially formed the EveryDay Angels Foundation, a nonprofit organization whose goal is to "foster honor and encourage everyday acts of kindness, beauty, and generosity," among other things.

Harris stresses that the foundation is not a

fan club. "The EveryDay Angels Foundation goes beyond Jewel and her music," he says. The foundation hopes to support worthy causes all over the country through extensive volunteer programs. "We want to make people aware that we are indeed each other's 'everyday angels.'"

The foundation also hopes to become a source of information for people who want to do something for others, but aren't sure where to start. "We will help identify things people can do, to make it as easy as possible" to find a way to help, Harris says.

There are not many performers who could inspire their fans to the degree that Jewel has. The very existence of the EveryDay Angels proves that Jewel is about much more than just selling records — a whole lot more.

# 8

## A Win, a Loss, and an Unforgettable Dress

If you're a musician and you're lucky, you get to make a living doing what you love. If you're even luckier, you get recognized for your talent. The entertainment industry gives out many awards each year. In the beginning of 1997, Jewel was up for two big ones.

First came the American Music Awards. Each year 20,000 fans choose the winners of the awards based on a list of nominees. In 1996, Jewel was up against Donna Lewis and No Doubt for Favorite New Pop-Rock Artist.

The ceremony was held January 27, 1997. Not only was it the first awards show Jewel had ever been to — it was the first one she had ever even seen! (No TV, remember?)

That night, Jewel found out just what a fan favorite she was. She won the award! In her acceptance speech, she said, "I know how little we can live with. I went from living in my car to this because you guys bought my album. It's because

40

you guys bought my album that I'm not stealing food."

Jewel barely had time to recover from the AMA ceremony before she had to get ready for another one — the Grammy Awards. In the music industry, winning a Grammy is the highest honor an artist can receive. Jewel was nominated in two categories: Best New Artist and Best Female Pop Vocal Performance.

"I really can't comprehend I'm up for a Grammy," Jewel told the *Bergen Record* before the big night on February 26, 1997. "It's something I didn't think about at all. I got into the music business because I wanted to live my dream."

On Grammy night, newcomer Jewel didn't win any awards. She lost Best New Artist to LeAnn Rimes. But, believe it or not, many of Jewel's fans were actually glad she lost that award. The *Orange County Register* explained, "Jewel went home empty-handed after being nominated for Best New Artist, which historically has been a kiss of death for musicians. Fans breathed a sigh of relief when she lost." (LeAnn Rimes probably shouldn't be worried, though; 1995's winner, Sheryl Crow, is doing just fine.)

After the show, however, people weren't talking about Jewel's loss. They were talking about something else — her dress.

*People* magazine described it as "a filmy Gianfranco Ferre dress." Others described the dress as, well, see-through. Whatever the case, the dress made a big splash in the press after the show. People just couldn't stop talking about it.

Did Jewel pick out a revealing dress on purpose? She told *Rolling Stone*, "I didn't know it was see-through. I tried it on in a hotel room. I haven't seen the pictures. I'm probably scared to."

In the *Boston Globe*, she explained, "You end up trying these things on in hotel rooms, which aren't backlit."

But in the same interview, Jewel defends the dress in another way. "I want to be allowed to experiment in front of the world. People were like, 'You can't be sexy and spiritual. You can't be sensitive and sexy.' But I refuse to be burdened by my womanhood."

Another person might have withered from all the attention, but not Jewel. "I'm brave in my living. I'll make mistakes. Like the dress for the Grammys," she later said in *Twist* magazine.

Jewel's sheer dress may have been an accident but, in the end, it couldn't do anything to take away from Jewel and her music. And it may even have earned her a few more fans!

# 9

# The Loves of Her Life

Jewel's love life is not something you're likely to read a lot about in magazines. The young singer has always been pretty quiet about her romances. But that doesn't mean she doesn't date. There have been a few guys who've made a difference in Jewel's life in one way or another.

Remember the rap group Jewel joined in ninth grade, La Creme? One of Jewel's first boyfriends was part of the group. Jewel told *Rolling Stone* that she dated a boy named Damien. Why did they break up? It might have something to do with the fact that Jewel left for Hawaii right after the time they were going out.

Jewel may have decided that she liked dating musicians. When she moved to San Diego, she met Steve Poltz, a member of the group the Rugburns. If you've ever seen the second "You Were Meant for Me" video, then you know what he looks like. He's Jewel's co-star.

Jewel met Poltz in 1992, when Jewel was

seventeen or eighteen and Poltz was thirty-two. The two started surfing together. But that wasn't the only thing they had in common. They had their music.

"Next thing I know, we started writing together," Poltz told *People* magazine. "There's just a cool chemistry we have . . . it's nice."

Poltz introduced Jewel to music she had never heard before — like the Beatles.

Jewel also picked up some songwriting tips from the seasoned musician. In *People* magazine, she admitted that Poltz is "the only person who, when he sings, makes me cry."

And in 1995, she told *Seventeen* magazine, "My boyfriend, Steve Poltz, is the best songwriter."

When Jewel was twenty-one, she told *This Is the Sound*, "There's a band called the Rugburns. Steve Poltz, their singer, has always been an influence."

After Jewel was discovered by Atlantic Records, she and Poltz were still collaborating. Besides "You Were Meant for Me," they also co-wrote the song "Adrian." And later, even after Poltz and Jewel broke up, they remained friends. The Rugburns would sometimes play with Jewel on tour.

The *Los Angeles Times* describes the Rugburns' sound as "modern folk, pop and rock full of unpredictable twists and turns."

*Daily Variety*, a key publication in the music industry, reviewed a 1997 Rugburns/Jewel show. "If Jewel proved anything at her two shows at the Wiltern, it was that the Rugburns should be her full-time backing band. . . . Beginning mid-set with "You Were Meant for Me," the doe-eyed love song that's currently the No. 3 single in the country, and which Jewel wrote with Rugburns frontman Steve Poltz, the show took on a new and exciting vibe."

While Jewel was making music with Steve Poltz, rumors were flying about her and a celebrity — Sean Penn. The actor is probably most famous for his role in *Fast Times at Ridgemont High* and for marrying and divorcing Madonna.

Penn first set eyes on Jewel during her star-making appearance on *Late Night With Conan O'Brien* in May 1995. Penn asked Jewel to write a song for a movie he was directing, *The Crossing Guard*. Jewel agreed and wrote "Emily." He was so impressed with her that he "began telling friends she was the next [Bob] Dylan," *Rolling Stone* reported.

In return, Penn directed a video for "You Were Meant for Me."

Gossip columns alleged that Jewel and the actor were dating; Jewel has always insisted the two were just good friends. The friendship doesn't seem to have lasted long. Penn went on to marry actress Robin Wright (of *Forrest Gump* fame). And Jewel shot a second video of "You Were Meant for Me." That's the version that stars Steve Poltz.

When this book went to press, Jewel was happy to admit to the press that she was dating Michel Francoeur, a French-Canadian male model. Are Jewel and Francoeur meant for each other? Only time will tell.

# 10

## A Very Good Year

For Jewel, 1996 was an incredibly eventful year, with *Pieces of You* hitting the charts and over 800 live performances. If it's possible, 1997 may have been filled with even more milestones for the singer. The year started off with Jewel's American Music Award for Favorite New Pop/Rock Artist and only got better and busier from there.

**February 1997**
- Jewel made her memorable appearance as a presenter at the Grammy Awards.

**March 1997**
- The Mediadome Web site presented a six-part "webisode" based on Jewel's life, music, and writings. Fans listened to music clips and wrote poetry inspired by Jewel's lyrics.

- On March 28, VH1 chose Jewel to debut its new show, *Hardrock Live.* Jewel sang ten songs during the hour, including some that fans had never heard before. Steve Poltz sang a duet with Jewel on "You Were Meant for Me." And fans were treated to two special numbers. Jewel called her dad on stage for a yodeling song, and sang a special version of "Rudolph, the Red-Nosed Reindeer" with her mom. *Variety* called the show an "engaging hour."

## May 1997

• Live, from New York, it's — Jewel! *Saturday Night Live* featured her as its musical guest on May 10.

• Jewel started her career as a magazine cover girl by gracing the cover of *Rolling Stone*.

## June 1997

• On June 12, Jewel brought the house down at the MTV Movie Awards by singing "Foolish Games." Believe it or not, the song does have a movie connection — you can find it on the soundtrack to *Batman and Robin*.

• Not to be outdone by VH1, MTV gave Jewel her own *Unplugged* special on June 24. In front of an audience at the Brooklyn Academy of Music, Jewel sang her hits "Who Will Save Your Soul," "Foolish Games," and "You Were

Meant for Me," as well as new songs "Satellite," "Passing Time," and "Too Darn Hot," a cover of a Cole Porter song.

## July 1997

• Jewel joined the Lilith Fair, an all-female tour featuring sixty-one different acts. The fair was the brainchild of Canadian singer Sarah McLachlan. The combination of Jewel, Tracy Chapman, Cassandra Wilson, Fiona Apple, Paula Cole, and many other headliners made the tour a critical and financial success. The first week of shows were all sellouts, and by the time the tour ended in August it had made more money than any other summer concert tour. Some of the proceeds of the concert tour went to charities.

The fact that the tour featured some of music's hottest acts and the hard work of organizer Sarah McLachlan is certainly responsible for the tour's success. But having Jewel on board certainly didn't hurt.

"Jewel, on the first and largest stage, was the high point. . . . In concert it [her voice] has a crackling, sparks-flying, campfire warmth," *Time* magazine reported.

MSNBC gave Jewel a glowing review after the July 5 show. "Arguably the evening's biggest attraction, Jewel took the stage in a show-stopping red evening gown and heels. Her generous, thirteen-song set demonstrated how far she has evolved since her best-selling debut album *Pieces of You*."

• On July 21, Jewel appeared on the cover of *Time* magazine. That honor has usually been reserved for world leaders and hard news stories. *Time* chose Jewel to illustrate the phenomenon of the popularity of strong women in the music industry. Also that month, Jewel made the covers of *Interview* and *Details* magazines.

• The next week, Atlantic Records released a limited-edition version of *Pieces of You*. The album was released on vinyl, not on CD, and featured five extra tracks: "Emily," "Rocker Girl," "Everything Breaks," "Cold Song," and "Angel Needs a Ride."

**September 1997**
• Jewel attended the MTV Music Video Awards. The singer took home a statue for Best Female Video for "You Were Meant for Me."

**October 1997**
• Atlantic Records announced that *Pieces of You* had gone platinum for the sixth time. Not bad for a folksinger!

- Jewel took her sound overseas on a tour of Asia and Europe. From October through November, Jewel performed in Taiwan, Japan, England, Scotland, France, Denmark, Norway, Sweden, Germany, Italy, Spain, Holland, Belgium, Ireland, and even Switzerland, the home of her ancestors. Jewel capped off the tour with a performance in London, and an attention-getting appearance on the National Lottery drawing, Britain's "most popular variety show."

## November 1997

- Jewel's official Web site, www.jeweljk.com, went online. Fans can log on to get the latest Jewel news, learn tour dates, buy merchandise, read an official biography, feast their eyes on pictures, and send E-mail to Jewel.

## December 1997

- *SWING* magazine named Jewel one of the thirty most powerful people in their twenties, along with Will Smith, Gillian Anderson, and Beck.

## What Does the Future Hold?

Jewel ended the year with a brief rest. When this book went to press, she was getting ready to sing the national anthem at the 1998 Super

Bowl — to be held in San Diego, the town where it all began for her.

She was discussing plans for the future. One thing she's been planning for a while is a second album.

The singer talked about it as early as 1996. "My next album will be more diverse," she told *Billboard*. "It will have some blues and jazz and more rock stuff, along with the acoustic stuff. It'll be kind of flirtatious, but not folk rock."

A year later, she told *Rolling Stone* that there may be a country song on the next album. She said that the next songs she's been working on have "a lot more layering. My hands have caught up to my head now."

The album may also feature an appearance from an old friend of Jewel's — the Red Hot Chili Peppers' Flea, who had faith in Jewel back when she was living in her van. Flea told MTV News that he would be lending his bass-playing skills to the disc.

*Billboard* reports that the album will be released in summer 1998.

Of course, hardworking Jewel won't just be recording in 1998. When this book went to press, *Variety* had just reported that Jewel was slated to star in the movie *To Live On*. Possible co-stars Tobey Maguire and Matt Damon could portray the two men in a love triangle with Jewel in the film, a Western set in the Civil War era. The movie will be based on the novel *Woe to Live On*, by David Woodrell.

We all know Jewel can sing, but can she act? So far, her biggest performance has been in the 1995 version of *The Wizard of Oz*. The *Daily News* had good things to say about her ability as an actress. "Her acting . . . is good throughout. She joins [Joel] Grey, [Debra] Winger, and [Nathan] Lane as the best dialogue performers in the cast." The paper didn't praise any of Jewel's fellow musicians in the cast for their acting, so it could be that Jewel really has something special going. She's already conquered music. Maybe the movie industry isn't far behind!

Whatever the future holds, Jewel is ready for it.

"Fans will come and go, and success will come and go," she mused in *Billboard* in 1996. "I don't want to live in my car again — I still worry about that. But I'll always have a purposeful drive, a passion. I live through my pen. It's how I experience the world."

It's that very drive and passion that are sure to take Jewel anywhere she wants to go.

# 11

## Straight from the Star's Mouth

Even though Jewel was only a tender twenty years old when she first caught the public eye, she came across as intelligent and mature. Jewel has been interviewed countless times, and she always has something interesting to say. Here's a look at Jewel's thoughts on a variety of subjects, in her own unmistakable words.

### Dealing with Fame
"I knew it was going to be like this. That's almost why I didn't do it." — The *Bergen Record*, 1995

"Sometimes my friends and I realize that people think I'm famous and we're, like, 'Weird!'" — *People,* 1997

### Sweet Success:
"The moment I can really remember is when I sold eight thousand records in one week. I re-

member crying on my kitchen floor, just thanking God that I might not ever have to waitress or live in my car again." — *Rolling Stone*, 1997

"Very few people get to live their passion. Some don't even know what their passions are. And that's very sad. I'm very lucky to be doing what I love." — The *Bergen Record*, 1995

**On Angels**
"It sounds so fluffy now, to believe in angels. Isn't it strange we begin to discredit what's popular?" — *Gannett News Service,* 1995

"We're constantly being bombarded with news of how mean we are to each other. And soon that's all we know. We become strangers to ourselves. A lot of people are brought up thinking they need to be forgiven just for being born. But really, we're our own angels, and we can answer prayers for each other." — *Billboard*, 1996

"I do believe in angels!" — to audience at the Beacon Theater, 1997

**On Innocence**
"Innocence needs to be maintained. I try not to be cynical . . . I learned at a really young age, you can get tough or you can let your innocence protect you." — *Newsday*, 1996

## Following Her Dream
"It wasn't until I got fired from my last job that I decided: That's it. I don't care. I'd rather die and drop out of the world rather than wake up every day and be so unhappy. I never thought I'd get a record deal. I just wanted to eat and do something I liked. It turned into this. And it's been a real blessing." — LAUNCHonline

"People shouldn't compromise their pride and health just to have roofs over their heads. And when you get to that point when you're willing to die for it, nothing else matters, you know?" — to Jon Stewart, guest host of the *Late Late Show With Tom Snyder*, 1997

## Musical Influences
"I'm not really a music fan. I don't listen to a lot of music, but Ella Fitzgerald I've really enjoyed." — *This Is the Sound*

## Advice to Fans
"Love bravely, live bravely, be courageous, there's really nothing to lose. There's no wrong you can't make right again, so be kinder to yourself, you know, have fun, take chances. There's no bounds." — *The Charlie Rose Show*

"People look at me in magazines and feel like I'm a phenomenon, as if what I've accomplished is beyond their ability. I tell them to knock it off. If you respect what I've done, then do something yourself." — *Time*, 1997

## Bad Habits?
"Well, I don't drink. I have problems with my kidneys, and it's never interested me, anyway." — *Rolling Stone*, 1997

## Participating in Democracy
"I'm very excited to vote. Collectively we will make a difference." — *Ladies' Home Journal*, 1996

## On One of Her Hobbies
"Horseback riding is the most natural thing in my blood — that and singing." — *Time*, 1997

## What She Believes
"I believe in charm . . . I believe in magic . . . I believe in hope." — *The Lauren Hutton Show*

## Who She Is
"I feel most myself when I'm on stage, when I'm singing, or when I'm writing." — *Rolling Stone*, 1997

## What She Wants to Be When She Grows Up
"What I am." — *This Is the Sound*

# 12

## Jewel's Personality Profile

To find out how Jewel's songs are selling, you can look on Billboard's music charts. But for a fun look at the forces at work shaping Jewel's personality, check out these astrological and numerological charts.

**Jewel's Star Chart**
Jewel's Birthdate: May 23, 1974
Astrological Sign: Gemini
Gemini Element: Air
Gemini Planetary Ruler: Mercury
Gemini symbol: the twins
Gemini motto: I can do anything
Gemini colors: yellow, orange
Gemini animal: monkey
May gemstone: emerald

**The Gemini Personality**
Gemini is one of the most artistic and creative signs of the zodiac. Ruled by Mercury, the planet

of communication, Geminis will use their creative abilities to reach out to the world. That's something Jewel does especially well with her music.

Like chattering monkeys, Geminis can be talkative, curious, and playful. Fans lucky enough to catch Jewel's live act can see this part of her personality in action, as she talks and jokes her way between songs.

Just like a spring breeze, airy Geminis are always on the move. That's certainly true of Jewel in recent years. She's been touring almost non-stop since 1995, and most recently took her act to Europe and Japan. Some Geminis are a little unfocused with this urge to travel and end up chasing after things that never materialize. So far, though, Jewel looks like she's on the right track!

The motto "I Can Do Anything" certainly rings true in Jewel's case. Not only is she a music superstar at the age of twenty-three, but she's pursuing acting as well. It looks like a successful film career could be in the stars for this versatile Gemini.

## Other Planets in Jewel's Chart

When Jewel was born, the planet Mercury was also in Gemini. Having both the sun and Mercury in Gemini strengthens Jewel's role as a communicator. It also means that Jewel is especially friendly and interested in all kinds of people.

The planet Mars was in Cancer when Jewel was born. Mars rules desire — the part of us that determines how we get what we want. Having Mars in Cancer means that Jewel will not hurt anyone or step on anyone's toes to get her way. Like her song says, she's sensitive, and always looking out for others.

The planet Venus rules love and relationships, and when Jewel was born it was in the sign of Aries. Aries is a sign of great passion. A Venus in Aries could mean that Jewel is a little bit of a flirt and that she's happiest when the person she's with is independent and not clingy.

### Other Famous People Who Share Jewel's Birthday
(Isn't it funny how many singers with one name were born on that day?)

Joan Collins, actress on *Dynasty*
Marvin Hagler, boxer
Drew Carey, actor and comedian
Shelley West, country singer
Phil Selway of Radiohead
Lorenzo, singer
Maxwell, singer

## Jewel's Numerological Profile

In numerology, number values are given to the letters in a person's name. Some people believe that those numbers can reveal things about that person's past, present, and future.

Judy Noll, an astrologer and numerologist who lives in London, England, figured out how the numbers add up in the name Jewel Kilcher. The chart shows several important time periods in Jewel's life. Between the ages of ten and fifteen, things may have been a little rough for Jewel emotionally, but the numbers show that she did have support and had chances to make her wishes come true. The ages sixteen and seventeen show a positive influence around the area of publishing, which in Jewel's case could refer to her songwriting, which she started polishing when she was at the Interlochen Center for the Arts.

At ages twenty and twenty-one the emphasis is on career-oriented travel. That makes sense, considering Jewel was twenty when her grueling tour schedule began. The numbers also show a secret romance during this time.

The beginning of 1997 ushered in a possibility of long-distance travel. Nineteen ninety-eight brings a good time for new business (a new album?). Financial endeavors will be successful!

The study of her name tells us these major points:

- Her motivation is to create social and personal harmony, to instill her ideas and principles in everyone else. She wants to right all wrongs.
- In her private dreamworld, she sees herself surrounded by peace, quiet, and beauty. She imagines people coming to her and sharing her wisdom with them.
- Her major talents lie in her ability to inspire confidence in people, her sincerity, her honesty, her perseverance, and her stubborn determination.
- She needs to expect travel, contacts, and change. Her emotional sensitivity may lead to a distress that she could describe as being in her soul.

When you combine her name with the numbers in her birthdate of May 23, 1974, it reveals the following:

- She has been given the challenge of handling her emotions. As much as she may insist she wants to stay sensitive and preserve her innocence, she is predestined to be challenged in that very area throughout her life.

• Her soul's destiny is to make her dreams a practical reality. She is destined to stand for the principle of faith, and she must be of strong character in order to organize her abstract imagination into practical, material things that others can use. Not only is she well equipped to follow her destined path, but she has tapped into a very effective way of doing exactly what her soul requires!

# 13
## Jewel from A to Z

If you turned to this chapter first, then you're probably the kind of no-nonsense person who likes to get the facts in one easy dose. You're in luck. Here's everything you need to know about Jewel, in convenient alphabetical order.

**A**
Alaska: Jewel's home state
"Amen": Jewel's favorite song on her album
American Music Awards: Jewel won best new pop/rock artist of 1996.
Atlantic Records: her record company
Atz Kilcher: her father, who taught her how to yodel

**B**
Birthday: May 23, 1974

**C**
*The Crossing Guard*: Jewel wrote the song "Emily" for the movie soundtrack.

# D

Dylan, Bob: Jewel toured with the rock legend in 1996.

Dyslexia: Jewel suffers from the disorder, which made it difficult for her to read.

# E

Etheridge, Melissa: The two performed in the VH1 special *Duets*.

EveryDay Angels: what Jewel's die-hard fans call themselves

# F

Fitzgerald, Ella: singer whose vocal stylings Jewel admired

Francoeur, Michel: the French-Canadian male model Jewel was dating as of December 1997

# G

Gemini: her astrological sign

Georgia: The state named May 23, Jewel's birthday, "Everyday, Angel Day."

Grammy Awards: Jewel was nominated for Best New Artist and Best Female Pop/Vocal Performance in 1996, but lost.

# H

Homer: Jewel grew up outside of this artsy little town in south central Alaska.

Homestead: The Kilchers worked and lived off the land there.


# I

Innerchange coffeehouse: where Jewel was playing when she was discovered by Atlantic Records

Interlochen Center for the Arts: the Michigan boarding school Jewel attended in eleventh and twelfth grades


# J

Java Joe's: the California coffeehouse where she first met previous boyfriend and collaborator Steve Poltz

Jazz: her horse

Jewelstock: the free concert Jewel gave in 1996 outside Woodstock, New York, for fans belonging to her online newsgroup


# K

Kilcher: Jewel's last name


# L

La Creme: the rap group Jewel belonged to in ninth grade

Lilith Fair: the all-female tour that featured Jewel, Fiona Apple, and Sarah McLachlan

**M**

Marble carving: one of Jewel's hobbies

MTV: Jewel has appeared on the channel in videos, awards shows, and in her very own *Unplugged* special.

**N**

Nedra Carroll: Jewel's mom, a glass artist. Mom and daughter once lived side by side in their vans in San Diego.

Neruda, Pablo: Jewel's favorite poet

**O**

Ottawa Indians: Jewel was briefly "adopted" into their tribe when she was in high school.

**P**

*Pieces of You*: her first album

Platinum: By the end of 1997, *Pieces of You* had gone platinum seven times.

**Q**

Quotable: Jewel has been interviewed on countless television shows and for newspapers and magazines.

**R**

Rugburns: San Diego band that sometimes performs with Jewel

# S

San Diego: the California city where Jewel lived after leaving Interlochen and where she was discovered

Star: Fans raised money to name a star after her: Jewel Kilcher — Star of the North.

Surfing: another one of Jewel's hobbies

# T

*Time* magazine: featured Jewel on its cover in July 1997

Tupperware: it's what she uses to hold soil from her Alaskan homestead to remind her of home

# U

Unplugged: MTV gave Jewel her own *Unplugged* special on June 24, 1997.

# V

Van: Jewel lived in one while struggling to make it as a singer in San Diego.

# W

Web site: Jewel's Web site is www.jeweljk .com

"Who Will Save Your Soul": Jewel's first hit single

*The Wizard of Oz*: a benefit performance on TNT in 1995 that starred Jewel as Dorothy

# X

"X"-boyfriend: Singer/songwriter Steve Poltz and Jewel met in San Diego and collaborated on the songs "You Were Meant for Me" and "Adrian."

# Y

Yodel: the Swiss singing style Jewel is known for

Yule Kilcher: Jewel's Swiss grandfather, who founded the family's Alaskan homestead

# Z

Zellweger, Renee: The *Jerry Maguire* star is a Jewel look-alike; the two are often mistaken for one another.

# 14

## Where to Find Jewel

If you want to contact Jewel, here are her snail mail and E-mail addresses. It's not likely that you'll get a personal reply, especially to E-mail, but you'll still get your message across!

**Jewel**
c/o Atlantic Records
9229 Sunset Blvd., Ste. 900
Los Angeles, CA 90069

**Jewel on the Web**
jeweljk@aol.com

The Internet is a great place to learn more about Jewel and to communicate with other fans. When this book went to press, these Web sites were all up and running. If you don't have any luck getting on them, here's a tip. Type in the address again, but leave off the information after the last backslash. You still may be able to reach the main page.

## The EveryDay Angels Foundation
When this book went to press, the foundation was just getting started. Board chairman Dennis Harris recommends doing a web search under "EveryDay Angels" to find their Web site, which he said would be up and running in early 1997.

## Atlantic Records Jewel Page
http://atlantic-records.com/nonframes/
  Artists_Music/news.html?artistID=39
Jewel's record company provides music clips, a bio, news, and tour information about the singer.

## Crash Boy's EDA Page
http://thespis.com/crashboy/
If you want to learn more about becoming an EveryDay Angel, then this is a great place to start. The easy-to-navigate site lets you know what the phenomenon is all about and provides links to other EDA pages. Fun fact: Crash Boy earned his nickname after crashing his car on the way home from the Jewelstock concert! (Don't worry — he's fine.)

71

## Jewel Kilcher on the World Wide Web
http:www.smoe.org/lists/jewels/angels/surf.html
A great source for links to other sites, with a detailed description of each one.

## Jewel's Official Website
http://www.jeweljk.com
Get the latest news, tour dates, and an official biography; buy merchandise; and send E-mail to Jewel.

## MTV/Yahoo UnfURLed Ultimate Artist Site
http://www.unfurled.com/ultimate_
   artists/jewel/index.html
Another great source for links to other Web sites, arranged by category.

## Jewelstock: Two Nights of Music for EveryDay Angels
http://www.theartof.com/jewelstock
Want the scoop on this legendary concert? Try here for a history and photos of the event.

## Rick Dees and the Weekly Top 40 Web Site
www.rick.com/chart.html
Track the progress of Jewel's singles and albums on this up-to-date source.

**Simply Jewel**
http://www.geocities.com/~simply_jewel/
This is one of the nicest fan sites out there, with a biography, facts, discography, and good links.

# 15
## Jewel's Discography

**Albums**

*Pieces of You*

(Atlantic Records, 1995)

1. "Who Will Save Your Soul"
2. "Pieces of You"
3. "Little Sister"
4. "Foolish Games"
5. "Near You Always"
6. "Painters"
7. "Morning Song"
8. "Adrian"
9. "I'm Sensitive"
10. "You Were Meant for Me"
11. "Don't"
12. "Daddy"
13. "Angel Standing By"
14. "Amen"

*Pieces of You* limited edition vinyl LP set
(Atlantic Records, 1997)
Includes all songs from the first album, plus five
   bonus tracks:
"Emily"
"Rocker Girl"
"Everything Breaks"
"Cold Song"
"Angel Needs a Ride"

## Soundtracks and Compilations
"Emily" — *The Crossing Guard* sound track
"Foolish Games" — *Batman and Robin* sound
   track
"Foolish Games" — *VH1 Crossroads*
"Have a Little Faith in Me" — *Phenomenon*
   sound track
"Sunshine Superman" — *I Shot Andy Warhol*
   sound track
"Under the Water" — *The Craft* sound track
"V-12 Cadillac" — *Music for Our Mother Ocean
   II*
The Wizard of Oz in Concert — *Dreams Come
   True*

## Special Promotions
(This is not a comprehensive list of all of Jewel's
promotional tapes, but you will find some of the
more interesting ones here.)

## 1996 Tour Three-Song Cassette Giveaway
This tape was given for free to the first 200 fans to arrive at each of Jewel's shows. It featured two songs by opening act Duncan Sheik, plus Jewel's own "Race Car Driver."

## Phyllis Barnaby Finally Gets a Bra
Atlantic Records released this uniquely titled promo tape, featuring "You Were Meant for Me," "Cold Song," "Rocker Girl," and "Emily."

## "Who Will Save Your Soul"/91X Interview
Features the single plus an almost-17-minute interview with radio host Mike Halloran.